THE AUTHORSHIP OF SHAKESPEARE

new Ⓑ 4 95

D0760685

The Authorship of Shakespeare

BY JAMES G. MC MANAWAY

FOLGER BOOKS

Published by
THE FOLGER SHAKESPEARE LIBRARY

Copyright © 1962 by the Folger Shakespeare Library.
All rights reserved.

Fourth printing 1974
Fifth printing 1979

The Folger Shakespeare Library is administered
by the Trustees of Amherst College.

LC 79-91457
ISBN 0-918016-25-8 (previously ISBN 0-8139-0091-3)
ISBN 0-918016-18-5 (Series)

Printed in the United States of America

"Hamlet. Why look you there. . . . My father in his
habit as he lived."

EVERY writer who wishes to write about the man William
Shakespeare longs, but longs in vain, to see him "in his habit
as he lived," to tell his story with the wealth of intimate detail
that is expected in the biographies of famous men. Nowadays
literary men and people of the theatre are idolized. Their voices
are on the radio, their faces on television and in the movies.
Their goings and comings are reported as news, and the public
knows, or thinks it knows, their tastes in breakfast food, bev-
erages, cigarettes, and women (or men, as the case may be).
They are public characters, lionized and, on occasion, mobbed
by ecstatic admirers.

To imagine a society in which there were no actresses, in
which actors were scarcely respectable, and in which literary
men were for the most part either wealthy amateurs or im-
poverished professionals—to imagine, in a word, the kind of
society in which Shakespeare lived—is difficult indeed.

For a playwright of his time, Shakespeare's life is well docu-
mented. He was christened on April 26, 1564, in Holy Trinity
Church, Stratford-upon-Avon, the eldest son to John and Mary
(Arden) Shakespeare; he died on April 23, 1616, and was
interred in the chancel of Holy Trinity Church. We know his
wife's name and origin, the dates of christening and burial of
their three children, as well as many facts of their later lives.
The elder daughter married the well-known Dr. John Hall and
in 1643 was hostess to the Queen of England, who spent two
nights and parts of three days at New Place, which Susanna

CONCORDIA UNIVERSITY LIBRARY
PORTLAND, OR 97211

Hall had inherited from her father. Susanna's daughter, Elizabeth, took for her second husband John Bernard, who was knighted by Charles II in 1661.

From the time that he began to enjoy prosperity—about 1596—William Shakespeare's financial dealings are recorded in some detail. He bought and restored New Place, the imposing house built about 1483 by Sir Hugh Clopton, mayor of Stratford. With his son's support, John Shakespeare secured the grant of arms for which application had been made earlier; thenceforth, each was *generosus*, a propertied gentleman. There were purchases of real estate in and about Stratford and, in 1613, in London. The London property was the Blackfriars Gatehouse, a logical purchase for a man whose company of actors had been performing in an adjacent Blackfriars building since 1609.

William Shakespeare, gent., of Stratford-upon-Avon, gave a deposition in a suit brought in 1612 by Stephen Belott to gain possession of the dowry promised Belott's wife, Mary Mountjoy, at the time of their marriage about 1603, when Shakespeare was lodging with the Mountjoys. His signature identifies him with the purchaser of the Blackfriars Gatehouse (two related documents bear his signature) and with the man who in the spring of 1616 signed the three pages of his will, bequeathing, among other things, twenty-six shillings and eight pence to his "fellows" Richard Burbage, John Heminges, and Henry Condell, to buy memorial rings. These men had been his fellow actors and friends since about 1594, and in 1623 Heminges and Condell brought out the First Folio edition of his plays "without ambition either of self-profit, or fame; only to keep the memory of so worthy a friend, and fellow alive, as was our Shakespeare."

Men of Shakespeare's age had a very different set of values from our own. Plays written for the public stage were not considered to be literature. *Nos haec novimus esse nihil:* "We know these things to be nothing," appears on the title page of one play quarto. The Latin motto expresses the opinion of many of the playwrights, who turned out scripts to be used by actors in the entertainment of a not always discriminating public.

Illus. 1(a). Shakespeare's signature to his deposition of May 11, 1612, in the Belott-Mountjoy lawsuit. From the original in the Public Record Office, London.

Illus. 1(b). Shakespeare's signature to the conveyance of the Gatehouse in Blackfriars, March 10, 1613. From the original in the Guildhall Library, London.

Illus. 1(c). Shakespeare's signature to the mortgage deed of the Gatehouse in Blackfriars, March 11, 1613. From the original in the British Museum.

The actors themselves led a precarious existence. A few gifted players who had business ability and prudence managed to become sharers in the ownership or operation of a playhouse and thus to acquire property and recognition as substantial citizens. Edward Alleyn, the great tragic actor of the Lord Admiral's Men, became wealthy enough to found Dulwich College. Heminges and Condell were churchwardens of St. Mary Aldermanbury in London. There is probably envy of their economic success mixed with scorn of their aspirations to gentility in the words that, about 1600, Ben Jonson puts into the mouth of one of his characters: "They [the actors] forget they are i' the statute, the rascals, they are blazoned there, there they are tricked, they and their pedigrees; they need no other heralds, I wis" (Tucca in *Poetaster* [I.ii.53 ff.]). The statute is that of 39 Elizabeth (1597–1598), ch. 4, where it is required that

[2] All fencers, bearwards, common players of interludes and minstrels wandering abroad (other than players of interludes belonging to any baron of this realm, or any other honorable personage of greater degree, to be authorized to play, under the hand and seal of arms of such baron or personage) . . . shall be taken, adjudged, and deemed rogues, vagabonds and sturdy beggars, and shall sustain such pain and punishment as by this Act is in that behalf appointed.

The initial punishment was that the culprit be

[3] stripped naked from the middle upwards and shall be openly whipped until his or her body be bloody [Sir Edmund Chambers, *The Elizabethan Stage* (Oxford, 1923), IV, 324].

Prosperity among actors was the exception. From the earliest times, minstrels, jugglers, and such entertainers of the public had been very low in the social scale, and it was with difficulty that they managed to rise in public esteem. A forceful character like Edward Alleyn or Richard Burbage might be sought after by certain of the young gentlemen of the Inns of Court and

4

celebrated in verse at his death. But their Bohemian way of life, the uncertainty of regular employment that was not lessened by frequent recurrences of the plague, which closed all places of entertainment, and the discomforts of taking to the road kept most actors outside the pale of respectability. This state of affairs continued until David Garrick proved later, in the eighteenth century, that an actor could live on terms of intimate friendship with the nobility. In the reigns of Elizabeth and James no one thought actors worthy of biographical notice.

Poets fared little better. Edmund Spenser, recognized by his contemporaries as the greatest nondramatic poet since Chaucer, writes that London was his "most kindly nurse," but the year of his birth is unknown, and although he claimed kinship with the great Spencer family of Althorpe, no one has discovered the nature of the relationship. His father's baptismal name is unknown; his mother's name is known only because the poet's praise of his second (or perhaps third) wife, Elizabeth Boyle, mentions the fact that Queen, mother, and wife shared the one name. There is no absolute certainty about the identity of Spenser's first wife. His early love, "Rosalind," is a mystery. There is only conjecture about what dashed his hopes of quasi-diplomatic service on the Continent. In Ireland, to which he seems to have been rusticated, he acquired property and became Clerk of the Council of Munster; but in 1581 he is also, mysteriously, prebendary of Effin. As clerk to Lord Grey, and in other official capacities, Spenser wrote many letters and documents, at least fifty-nine of which have been identified. They are written in three distinct hands: two for English (secretary and italic) and one for Latin. No personal letter to or from him has come to light and not one line of poetry in his handwriting.

John Milton, who was born in 1608 a few years before Shakespeare's death and who lived till 1674, was famous as a poet and political writer. He was the first great English poet to have his biography written by his contemporaries, but the first life of Milton to appear independently was composed by one

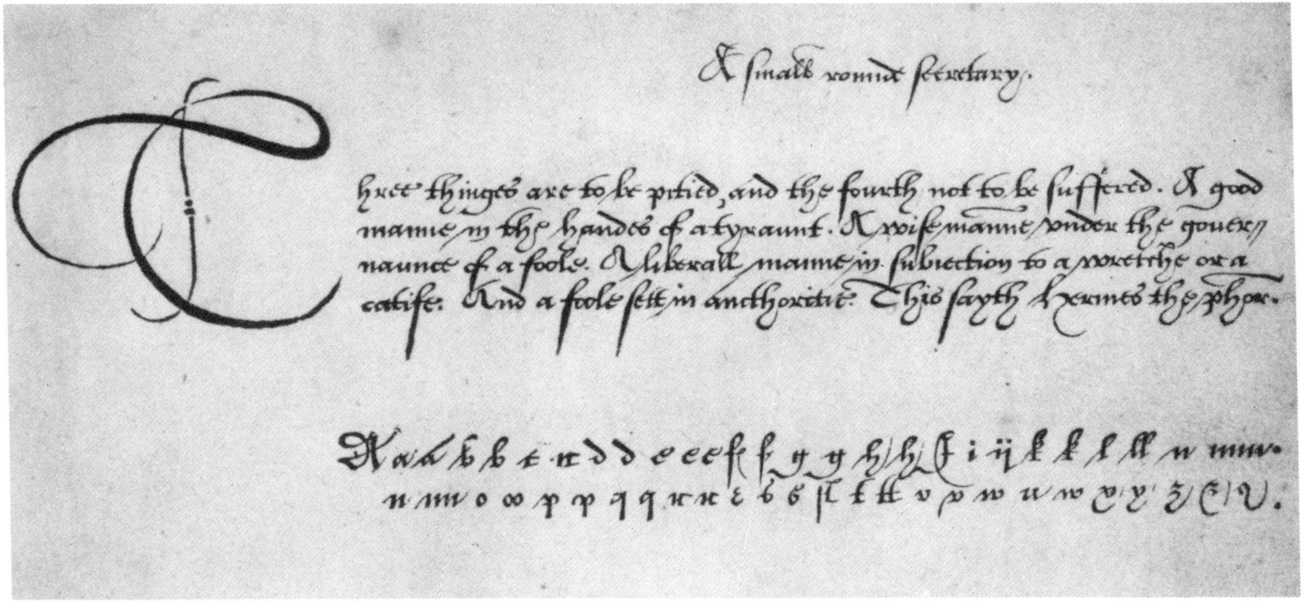

Illus. 2. "A small rounde secretary. Three thinges are to be pitied, and the fourth not to be suffered. A good manne in the handes of a tyraunt. A wise manne vnder the gouernaunce of a foole. A liberall manne in subiection to a wretche or a catife. And a foole sett in auchoritie. This sayth Hermes the ph[i]losophlor." Example of secretary hand. From Jean de Beauchesne and John Baildon, *A New Book, Containing All Sorts of Hands Usually Written at This Day in Christendom, as the English and French Secretary* (London, 1611).

of his adopted nephews (Edward Phillips) not because Milton was a poet but because he had written a violent political book while serving as Latin secretary during the Commonwealth period. Yet with all the autobiographical publicity that accompanied Milton's bitter pamphlet war with foreign critics of England, the cause of his rustication from Cambridge is unknown, and the facts of his unhappy first marriage are still a mystery. It was to be expected that Milton would lose his life, along with the regicides, when Charles II came to the throne in 1660; but while his friends spirited the blind poet away from London, Andrew Marvell interceded for him in Parliament, and the Royalist Sir William Davenant (whom Milton is reported to have saved from execution about 1651) obtained his release. "The details," writes a recent biographer, "remain obscure."

It is instructive to note that in William Winstanley's *England's Worthies* (1660) the two Elizabethan poets Sir Philip Sidney and John Donne are included because the first was the flower of chivalry (there is a brief reference to the *Arcadia* and to the *Astrophel and Stella*) and the second was dean of St. Paul's (there is one reference to a religious poem).

That blazing star, Sir Walter Raleigh, illustrates well the indifference of his age to biography and to literary manuscripts. A well-known editor of his poems writes of him:

Raleigh was born about 1552, at Hayes Barton in Devonshire. . . . Some time in his teens he went up to Oriel College, Oxford, where it is not recorded that he took a degree. . . . Of the next ten years, the formative years of his life, we know very little beyond the fact that he fought in the French Wars of Religion and in the Irish campaigns of Lord Grey. . . . There is more than one story that professes to account for his sudden rise to favour, but they are fairy-tale chances and lean on the logic of day-dreams [Agnes M. C. Latham, ed., *The Poems of Sir Walter Raleigh* (London, 1951), p. xv].

The date of his birth is uncertain; the name of the school he attended is unknown. There is a decade of which research has discovered almost nothing. This is the man who for ten years was a reigning favorite at Court, a great sea captain, the adventurer who sank £40,000 of his private fortune in attempts to colonize Virginia, the man who is credited with introducing tobacco into England and the potato into Ireland. He was envied and hated by the greatest in England. His *History of the World*, written while he was a prisoner in the Tower, went through ten editions between 1611 and 1700. Some autograph letters survive, but not one manuscript page of *The History of the World*. Of his poetical works, a fragment of *Cynthia*, 522 lines, in his handwriting, is among the Cecil Papers at Hatfield House; and the late W. A. White is reported to have had a two-page autograph manuscript of "The Lie." No one troubled to preserve the original manuscripts of anything else that he is known to have written.

The author of the Jacobean tragedies that rank nearest to Shakespeare's was John Webster. Here is a biographical note about him published in 1941:

Of the Elizabethan dramatists there is not one concerning whose life we know less than John Webster's. Hitherto antiquarian research has failed to bring to light any biographic data of any consequence. We do not know when or where he was born or died, who his parents were, what sort of education he received, whether he really was a tailor by trade, whether he was married, how he earned his living, and so forth [S. A. Tannenbaum, *John Webster (A Concise Bibliography)* (New York, 1941), p. vii].

The other playwrights of the time are little better known to us, with the exception of Christopher Marlowe and Ben Jonson, and there are special reasons why so much is recorded about them. The parish registers and school records of Canterbury, where Marlowe, the son of a shoemaker, was born, have been preserved. He won a scholarship and matriculated at Corpus Christi College, Cambridge, from which he received the degree of Master of Arts in mysterious circumstances. Something of his later life is recorded because of a killing in which he became involved, because of his outspoken, unorthodox opinions about religion, but most of all because of his violent death. About Jonson, whose stepfather was a bricklayer, considerably more is known, but even of this pugnacious man's biography many details are in question. He was born in 1572, possibly on June 11. His father was probably a clergyman, but his baptismal name is unknown; neither the baptismal name nor the surname of the mother is recorded. In 1589 Jonson was withdrawn from Westminster School, to which he had been sent by "a friend," and "put to another craft." And in July, 1597, "he makes his sudden appearance in Henslowe's employ." In the "lost years" he had service (dates unknown) in the wars in the Low Countries, where he won a duel and stripped his dead foe. Of his long-suffering wife, the one recorded fact is that she and her husband were subject to "correction" in 1606 for habitually absenting themselves from service and communion in the parish church. The couple had at least two children, Mary, who lived only six months, and Ben, who died in 1603 at the age of seven. Jonson fought another duel, with a fellow actor, and escaped execution only by pleading benefit of clergy. (In medieval times the clergy were permitted to plead exemption from sentence for having committed certain felonies; later, this privilege—not abolished until 1827—was extended to any first offender who could read. The test passage, often called the neck verse, was usually a Latin version of Psalm 51 printed in black letter.) Most of the known details of his later life have been preserved because of his irregularity in religion, his association with the nobility while writing court masques, and his aggressiveness in every relationship. His part in writing a play, *The Isle of Dogs*, landed him in prison in 1597, and he was in prison again in 1604 for his part in *Eastward Ho*. Jonson was at the center of the War of the Theatres in 1599–1602; he quarreled with Inigo Jones about court masques; and he was contemptuous in criticism of contemporary writers and dictatorial in stating his own literary theories. In short, Marlowe and Jonson had color; they made news. Their lives were filled with actions that brought them in conflict with authority and thus into the kinds of official records that have been preserved.

The other playwrights of the time led less violent lives and, consequently, are shadowy figures. Of John Lyly, Thomas Lodge, George Peele, Thomas Dekker, Robert Greene, Samuel Daniel, George Chapman, and Thomas Heywood, for example, the year of birth can only be guessed. No autograph of Robert Greene has been discovered. Of the others named, there are a few signatures, an autograph letter or two, but no literary autographs except a scrap from Marlowe, a fragment of a poem of Daniel's, an autograph poem by Peele, and lines in *Sir Thomas More* in Dekker's hand. These men are better known to us than Webster, less known than Marlowe and Jonson.

Shakespeare lived quietly, unobtrusively, for the most part—there are many contemporary references to "gentle" Shakespeare. He fought no duels, had no religious difficulties, served no time in jail for debt or violence, avoided dogmatism in literary matters, wrote no court masques. He did not make news or get into official records in the same way that Marlowe and Jonson did.

The first English playwright to have a formal biography written to be published with his *Works* was William Shakespeare. For his edition of the plays in 1709, the first modern edition of an English playwright, Nicholas Rowe collected what data he could in London and then sent the famous Shakespearean actor Thomas Betterton (1635?–1710) to Stratford to look at records there, such as the parish registers, and to collect local traditions of Shakespeare. Betterton began acting *Hamlet* in 1660 and continued to play the title role and other Shakespearean roles until 1709. His career began while William Beeston and the younger William Cartwright were still active in the theatres. Pepys saw Cartwright play Falstaff in 1667. Both Beeston and Cartwright had been actors before the Puritans closed the playhouses in 1642. The elder William Cartwright was an actor with the Lord Admiral's Men, chief rivals to

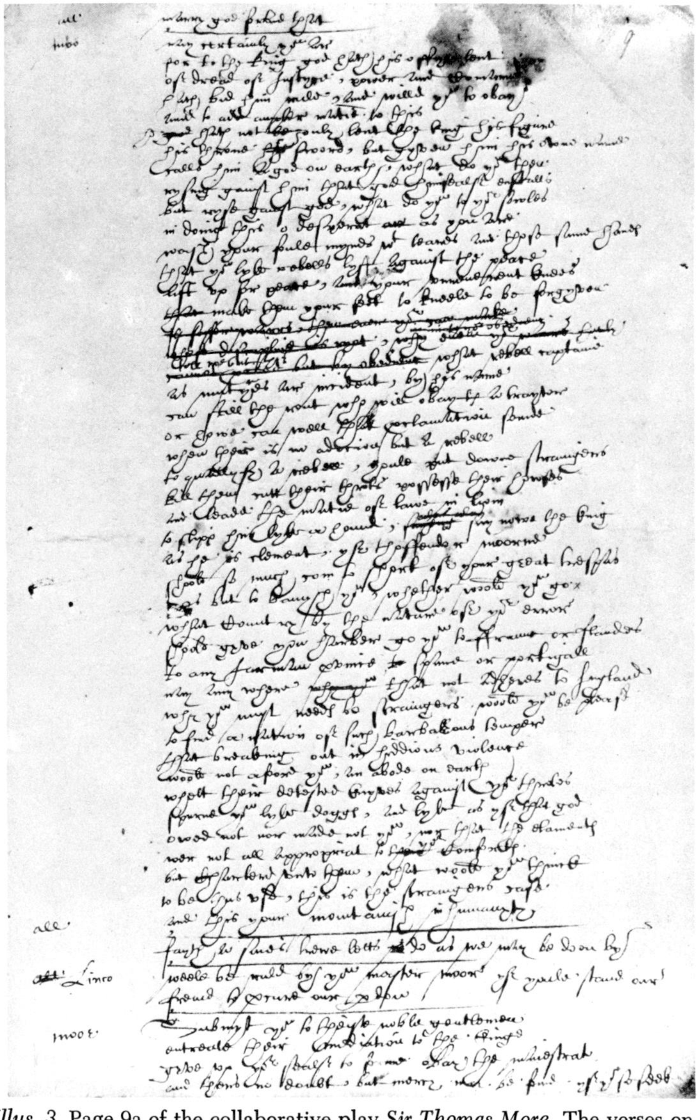

Illus. 3. Page 9a of the collaborative play *Sir Thomas More*. The verses on pages 8a, 8b, and 9a are thought by many to be in the handwriting of William Shakespeare. From the original in the British Museum (Harleian MS 7368).

Shakespeare's company; and Beeston's father Christopher was a fellow member of Shakespeare's company in 1598. They knew Shakespeare, and their sons knew of him. About 1681 William Beeston told John Aubrey, among other things, that Shakespeare had been a schoolmaster. He was also Aubrey's authority for the statement that Shakespeare was "the more to be admired *quia* [because] he was not a company keeper; lived in Shoreditch; wouldn't be debauched. And if invited to, wrote [that] he was in pain." In other words, Shakespeare did not care for drunken riots and, if invited, pleaded a headache. He could put into Falstaff's mouth the praise of sherry sack, but his own opinion seems to have been more like that of Cassio: "O God, that men should put an enemy in their mouths to steal away their brains! That we should, with joy, pleasance, revel, and applause, transform ourselves into beasts!"

Another man from whom Betterton learned about Shakespeare was Sir William Davenant (1606–1668), who was writing plays in 1634 and managed the Duke's Company after 1660. He it was who instructed Betterton in how Shakespeare had taught Burbage to play Prince Hamlet. Davenant was godson to Shakespeare and, in his cups, suggested that the relationship might be closer. His elder brother, Robert, who became an eminent divine, said in Aubrey's hearing that when he was a small boy (he was born in 1603) Shakespeare "gave him a hundred kisses." For a hundred years after Shakespeare's death there was an unbroken tradition among playwrights and theatre people, who knew him "indirectly, and directly too." These were the people in the best position to know the facts, and they accepted without question the fact that Shakespeare the actor was the poet and playwright.

Against this background of Shakespeare's biography and reputation it is desirable now to place some of the particular details of his life, beginning with his education and following with some of the recorded facts of his life in London and of his literary career.

The law of the universe seems to be that everything changes.

Men establish new forms of government—republics instead of absolute monarchies; scientists prove that the earth moves around the sun and then relate our galaxy to the countless other galaxies in space; biologists and psychologists discover some of the marvels of the human body and mind; and the new learning displaces the old. Systems of education are revolutionized. Latin, the universal language, once the most important subject for study from primary school to the university, is now read with pleasure by very few people, and spoken by still fewer. Literary classics written in former times seem difficult and a little strange. The plays of Shakespeare have suffered this fate. The ideas about physiology and psychology current in his day seem quaint. Stories that he borrowed from Ovid, his references to characters in classical myth, give his lines now an appearance of erudition. How amazed he would be to hear a modern ten-year-old prattle about jet propulsion and trips to the moon! Other times, other customs; the commonplaces of one age are marvels to another.

What appears to modern readers as great learning in Shakespeare was more justly appraised by his contemporaries and by those in succeeding generations who attended similar grammar schools and had, besides, the advantages of university education. In *The Progress to Parnassus*, a play written by Cambridge students about 1601, the character called "Kempe" (after Will Kempe, the comic actor in Shakespeare's company) says to "Burbage": "Few of the university men pen plays well, they smell too much of that writer Ovid, and that writer Metamorphoses, and talk too much of Proserpina and Jupiter. Why here's our fellow Shakespeare puts them all down, I [aye] and Ben Jonson too." Ben Jonson told the Scotch poet William Drummond that "Shakespeare wanted art." Francis Beaumont's poetical letter from the country to Jonson is more explicit:

> Here I would let slip
> (If I had any in me) scholarship,
> And from all learning keep these lines as clear

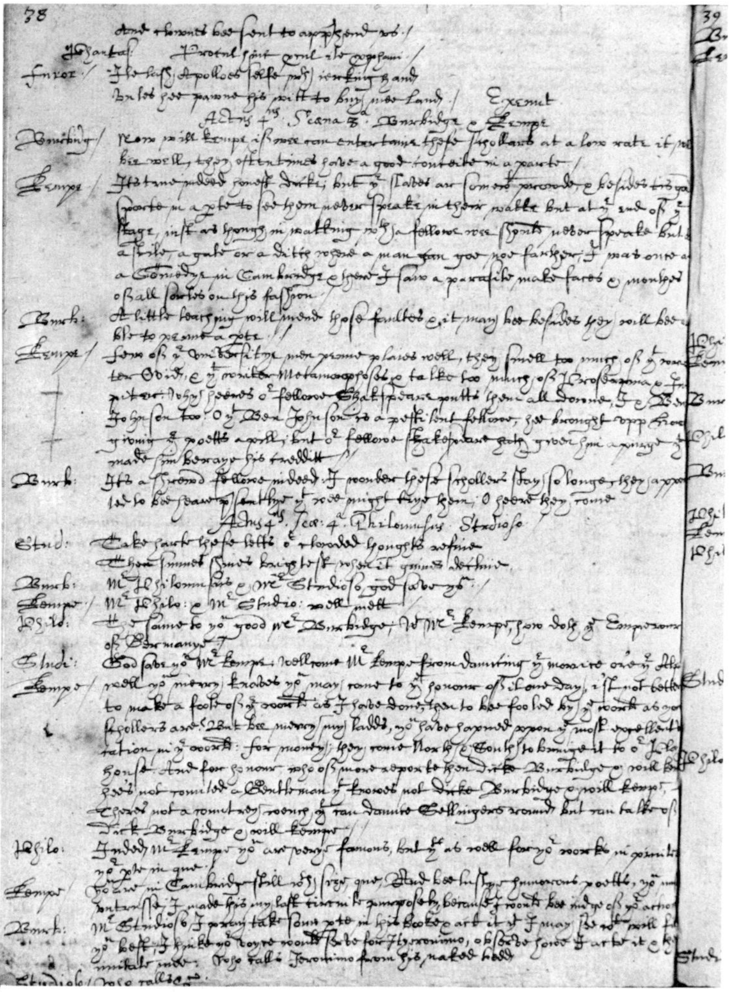

Illus. 4. A page of *The Progress to Parnassus*, "as it was acted in St. John's College in Cambridge, Anno 1601." An anonymous play, written and performed by students at Cambridge. Folger MS V.a. 355. The cross in the margin is opposite the reference to Shakespeare quoted on page 13.

As Shakespeare's best are, which our heirs shall hear
Preachers apt to their auditors to show
How far sometimes a mortal man may go
By the dim light of Nature.

Thomas Fuller, in his *Worthies, Warwickshire* (1662), compares Shakespeare to Plautus, "who was an exact comedian, yet never any scholar," and adds boldly: "Indeed his [Shakespeare's] learning was very little." A paragraph in Nicholas Rowe's "Life" that prefaced his edition of Shakespeare in 1709 puts the matter admirably. Rowe was poet laureate, a writer of successful plays, a friend of Addison and Pope, and a beneficiary of the Prince of Wales's generosity. Among the bits of information he gleaned about Shakespeare, probably through Betterton's inquiries at Stratford, is a direct statement about Shakespeare's schooling.

His father, who was a considerable dealer in wool, had so large a family, ten children in all, that tho' he was his eldest son he could give him no better education than his own employment. He had bred him, 'tis true, for some time at a free school, where 'tis probable he acquired that little Latin he was master of; but the narrowness of his circumstances, and the want of his assistance at home, forc'd his father to withdraw him from thence, and unhappily prevented his further proficiency in that language. It is without controversy that he had no knowledge of the writings of the ancient poets, not only from this reason, but from his works themselves, where we find no traces of anything that looks like an imitation of 'em; the delicacy of his taste and the natural bent of his own great genius, equal, if not superior to some of the best of theirs, would certainly have led him to read and study 'em with so much pleasure that some of their fine images would naturally have insinuated themselves into and been mix'd with his own writings; so that his not copying at least something from them may be an argument of his never having read 'em. Whether his ignorance of the ancients were a disadvantage to him or no may admit of a dispute; for tho' the knowledge of 'em might have made him more correct, yet it is not improbable but that the regularity and deference for them which would have attended that correct-ness might have restrain'd some of that fire, impetuosity, and even beautiful extravagance which we admire in Shakespeare: and I believe we are better pleas'd with those thoughts, altogether new and uncommon, which his own imagination supplied him so abundantly with, than if he had given us the most beautiful pas-sages out of the Greek and Latin poets, and that in the most agree-able manner that it was possible for a master of the English lan-guage to deliver 'em. Some Latin without question he did know, and one may see up and down in his plays how far his reading that way went. In *Love's Labor's Lost,* the pedant comes out with a verse of Mantuan, and in *Titus Andronicus,* one of the Gothic princes, upon reading

Integer vitae scelerisque purus
Non eget Mauri jaculis nec arcu—

says, "Tis a verse in Horace," but he remembers it out of his gram-mar, which, I suppose, was the author's case.

What is known of Shakespeare's education comes, then, largely from the poems and plays themselves. The Stratford of his boyhood was blessed with a good grammar school refounded under the charter of 1553 from Edward VI. Its master was paid £20 a year and provided with a house. This equaled the salary of the master of Eton and enabled the borough to employ first-class men. Thomas Jenkins, for example, who was master from 1575 to 1579, the years when young William should have been in the upper school, was fellow or scholar of St. John's College, Oxford, B.A. April 6, 1566, M.A. April 8, 1570. A high-school principal of equivalent education today would be a Ph.D. of Harvard.

The registers of the school are not extant, but it is incredible that William Shakespeare was not one of the pupils. His father was an energetic and ambitious man. A relative newcomer to Stratford, he was chosen a member of the borough council in 1557. Five years later he served two years as one of the two chamberlains, and upon the expiration of his term he was charged with preparing the borough accounts during the two-

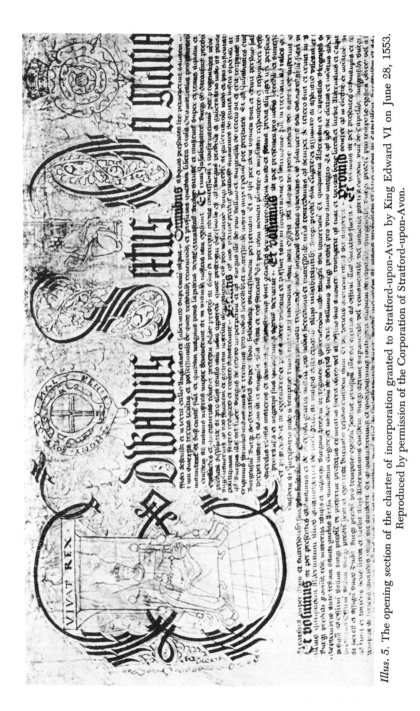

Illus. 5. The opening section of the charter of incorporation granted to Stratford-upon-Avon by King Edward VI on June 28, 1553. Reproduced by permission of the Corporation of Stratford-upon-Avon.

year term of the men who followed him in office. In 1568 he was elected to the highest municipal office, that of high bailiff. His application for a grant of arms in 1576 shows his aspirations. Such a man would never deny his first-born son the privilege of schooling to which his father's position entitled him.

Passages in several of the plays show intimate knowledge of the books that were used in the lower and upper schools of England. The hornbook, from which the children learned their letters, is twice referred to (*Love's Labor's Lost* [V.i.48]; *Richard III* [I.i.54–57]). Next came the *ABC with the Catechism*, alluded to in *King John*, "And then comes answer like an Absey book" (I.i.196), and *The Two Gentlemen of Verona* (II.i.22). There are frequent quotations from the Psalms, regularly in the version found in the Book of Common Prayer, which in some schools replaced the usual primer. From each of these, boys learned selections from the services of the church, certain prayers, and passages from the Scriptures. These books were the chief texts of the petty school; when committed to memory, as they had to be, they stored the pupils' minds with the best English prose, the great poetry of the Psalms, and the fundamentals of Anglican religion.

At the age of about six William should have entered grammar school, where he would have been expected to learn to read and write Latin easily and to speak it. The important text was Lily's *A Short Introduction of Grammar*, printed largely in Latin. It is named in one of the earliest plays, *Titus Andronicus* (IV.ii.20–23), where two lines are quoted from Horace. In the *Sententiae pueriles* of Culmannus and the *Disticha moralia* of Cato with notes by Erasmus a boy found moral maxims and explicit warnings against vice. Other maxims were committed to memory from the *Adagia* and *Apopthegmata*, in which were found many of the best lines from the Greek and Roman writers. *Aesop's Fables*, a play or two from Terence and Plautus, Mantuan's *Eclogues* (see reference in *Love's Labor's Lost* [IV.ii.95–96], the *Zodiacus vitae* of Palingenius, and Nowell's *Catechism*, which was studied in English, Latin, and Greek, gave the grammar-school boys more and better Latin than all but a few college students now possess. And the intensive method of teaching fixed the religious and profane texts indelibly in young memories. The oral and written exercises imparted skill in rhetoric and stretched the imagination, as the boys practiced writing letters and delivering orations, taking care always to choose sentiments appropriate to the given situation and words suitable to the writer or speaker. Ovid, Virgil, Cicero, Horace, and Juvenal gave schoolboys a familiarity with classical mythology that in these days, when even the modern languages are studied with reluctance, would be expected only in college courses in Latin. The textbooks of the petty and the grammar school were the ones that Shakespeare knew. The curriculum of the universities was a closed book to him.

Shakespeare's education was one of the topics about which John Aubrey questioned William Beeston, and this is his memorandum: "Though as Ben Jonson says of him, that he had but little Latin and less Greek, he understood Latin pretty well: for he had been in his younger years a schoolmaster in the country." Such a youthful occupation is entirely compatible with scenes in several early plays. Holofernes in *Love's Labor's Lost* is described as a pedant, who teaches the *ABC*, and there is much schoolboy punning on Latin words. In *The Taming of the Shrew* Lucentio disguises himself as a tutor so that he may court Bianca, and there is a short burlesque of a Latin lesson ([III.i]; Tranio has already quoted Lily's *Grammar* at I. ii.167). Another tutor, Sir Hugh Evans, is introduced in *The Merry Wives of Windsor*, and when William recites his elementary Latin there is much laughter at Mistress Quickly's ignorance (IV.i). The good humor with which pedagogues are treated shows that though Shakespeare may have crept unwillingly to school he had vivid—and fond—recollections of his experiences.

Once the limits of Shakespeare's formal education are recognized, it is easier to see the qualities that make his writings immortal. He read books in London, read them avidly and efficiently, taking from them stories for his plays and ideas for his characters, but he was not bookish. "Small have continual plodders ever won," says Biron in *Love's Labor's Lost,* "save base authority from others' books." A main part of Shakespeare's genius lay in his possession of a quality that his Julius Caesar attributes to Cassius: "He is a great observer, and he looks quite through the deeds of men." Not for him the simplicity of King Duncan, who reflects sadly, "There's no art to find the mind's construction in the face." Better than any other poet, Shakespeare could listen to a voice, regard a face, and, in imagination, conjure up the thoughts and emotions of all kinds of people, low and high. The other part of his genius was in his ear for the rhythms of speech and his matchless use of words.

The year of Shakespeare's arrival in London is unknown, as are the circumstances that brought him. Whether he was a private tutor, as Beeston reported, or simply a young man with a family to support and the consciousness of a gift of poetry, he must shortly have become an actor and a playwright. For by 1592 he was vilified in a posthumous book by Robert Greene for his presumption in writing plays. When powerful friends came to his defense, Henry Chettle, Greene's literary executor, published an apology: "My self have seen his demeanor no less civil than he excellent in the quality he professes: Besides, divers of worship have reported his uprightness of dealing which argues his honesty, and his facetious grace in writing, that approves his art." This means that Shakespeare was thus early a good actor ("the quality he professes") and a successful writer, that he conducted himself like a gentleman ("uprightness"; "honesty"), and that he had won the favor and friendship of people of high station ("divers of worship").

When the plague closed the playhouses in 1592–1594, he had time to write—or at least to publish—two narrative poems, *Venus and Adonis* (1593) and *The Rape of Lucrece* (1594), the only books he saw through the press. Each of these is

dedicated to the young Earl of Southampton, who may plaus-
ibly be identified as one of the "divers of worship."

The popularity of Shakespeare's plays that made Greene
envious led publishers to buy his play manuscripts whenever
they could. *Titus Andronicus* appeared in print in 1594. Unauthorized texts of *Henry VI, Part 2* and *Part 3*, were published
in 1594 and 1595 as *The First Part of the Contention of . . .
York and Lancaster* and *The True Tragedy of Richard Duke of
York*. By 1598 publishers began to put Shakespeare's name on
title pages: *Richard II* (quartos 2 and 3), *Love's Labor's Lost*,
and *Richard III* (quarto 2). Before this time the public had
paid little attention to the authorship of plays.

In this same year 1598 Londoners could read in *Palladis
Tamia, Wits Treasury*, a description of the state of English
poetry. The author, Francis Meres, probably taking a hint
from Richard Carew's *The Excellence of the English Tongue*
(ca. 1596), in which Shakespeare had been compared to
Catullus, names the important English writers beginning with
Chaucer and equates each with one of the classical authors.
Meres's purpose was to proclaim that the English language was
a suitable medium for good writing and that England had poets
equal to the best of other lands. Incidentally, he names twelve
plays by Shakespeare.

Meres lists Shakespeare as a distinguished writer of many
kinds of literature: he names him along with Sidney and
Spenser as an enricher of the English language; with Spenser
and Daniel as a lyric poet; with Lord Buckhurst, Dr. Legge,
Dr. Edes, and Marlowe as a writer of tragedies; with the Earl
of Oxford, Dr. Gager, Rowley, and Lyly as a writer of
comedies; and with the Earl of Surrey, Sir Thomas Wyatt, Sir
Philip Sidney, Spenser, and Drayton as "the most passionate
among us to bewail and bemoan the perplexities of love." "The
Muses," he writes, "would speak with Shakespeare's fine filed
phrase, if they would speak English." As for drama in general,
"As Plautus and Seneca are accounted the best for Comedy

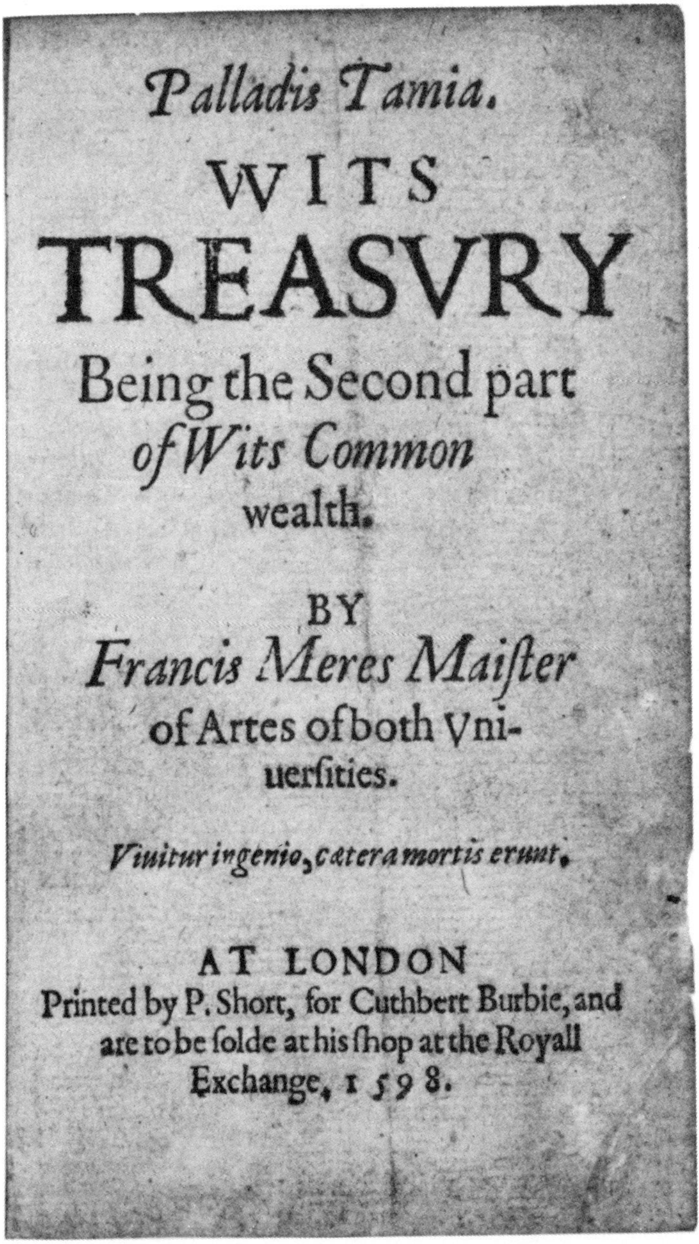

Palladis Tamia.

WITS
TREASVRY

Being the Second part
of *Wits Common*
wealth.

BY
Francis Meres Maister
of Artes of both Vni-
uerſities.

Viuitur ingenio, cætera mortis erunt.

AT LONDON
Printed by P. Short, for Cuthbert Burbie, and
are to be ſolde at his ſhop at the Royall
Exchange, 1 5 9 8.

Illus. 6. Title page of *Palladis Tamia.* The work contains a description of English poetry in Shakespeare's time.

and Tragedy among the Latins; so Shakespeare among the English is the most excellent in both kinds for the stage."

This testimony of Meres is invaluable, not only because it names twelve of Shakespeare's plays then in existence and mentions that his sonnets were circulating in manuscript among his private friends, but because it represents the knowledge of a hack writer, familiar with all the gossip of literary London. A master of arts of both universities, Meres came to London and began a literary career. Between 1595 and 1602 he published a sermon, translated a devotional book, and had a share in the production of a series of anthologies. In 1602 he was named rector of Wing in Rutland and removed from London.

Three things make Meres's record important: (1) he names the poets in each group in order of social rank: earls, barons, knights, doctors, gentlemen, common people; (2) writing while most of the men were still living, he mentions both the Earl of Oxford and Shakespeare in one group: "The best for Comedy amongst us be, Edward Earl of Oxford, Doctor Gager of Oxford, Master Rowley once a rare scholar of learned Pembroke Hall in Cambridge [of which Meres was B.A.], . . . Lodge, . . . Shakespeare . . . "; and (3) Meres moved in the same circles as many of the poets. Nicholas Ling, who collected the first volume of the series of anthologies to which Meres contributed the second, was the publisher of the first and second quartos of *Hamlet* (1603, 1604/1605), and James Roberts, the printer of Volumes I and III of the series and also the first quarto of *The Merchant of Venice*, quarto 2 of *Titus Andronicus*, and quarto 2 of *Hamlet*, had a contract with the Lord Chamberlain's men, Shakespeare's company, to print their playbills; he also made a series of staying entries for them in the Stationers' Register. Roberts, Ling, and, consequently, Meres were in a position to know Shakespeare personally, both as actor and playwright.

Shortly after his arrival in London to ascend the throne of England, King James took under his protection the Lord Chamberlain's Men, who were thenceforth known as the King's Men. The license, dated May 19, 1603, begins thus: "We . . . do license and authorize these our servants Lawrence Fletcher, William Shakespeare, Richard Burbage, Augustine Phillips, John Heminge, Henry Condell . . . to use and exercise the arts and faculty of playing comedies, tragedies, histories . . . during our pleasure." And pursuant to this appointment Shakespeare was one of those to whom four yards of red cloth were issued by the Master of the Great Wardrobe, to walk (or ride) in procession with the King through London on March 15, 1604. This is only one of the documents that link Shakespeare and Heminges and Condell.

The fortunate discovery in the Public Record Office of some of the documents in a suit brought in 1612 by Stephen Belott against his father-in-law, Christopher Mountjoy, a Huguenot refugee, provides a positive link between Stratford and London. The details of the suit are relevant only to the extent that they prove Shakespeare's acquaintance with the Mountjoy family in 1602 and his dwelling in their house, at least for a time, in 1604, where he might have improved his knowledge of French. One of the documents is a deposition by William Shakespeare of Stratford-upon-Avon, gentleman, of the age of forty-eight years or thereabouts, the signature to which corresponds to those on Shakespeare's will.

On March 10, 1613, Shakespeare bought of Henry Walker a house in Blackfriars known as the Gatehouse. The conveyance, bearing Shakespeare's signature, is in the Guildhall Library, London; the counterpart, signed by Walker, is in the Folger Shakespeare Library. Shakespeare is identified as a gentleman of Stratford-upon-Avon. Associated with him in the transaction were John Heminges, gentleman, William Johnson, vintner, and John Jackson, gentleman, all of London. Heminges, Jackson, and Johnson were trustees for Shakespeare. The purchase price was £140. Heminges is the fellow actor named in the King's warrent of 1604 who would help bring out the Folio of 1623. William Johnson has been identified as the owner of the famous Mermaid Tavern in Bread Street. John Jackson, gentleman, was a well-to-do Londoner from Kingston-upon-Hull, who in 1599 had acted as a trustee for Shakespeare and the other members of his company in distributing the shares in the ground lease of the Globe. Another document relating to the property, a mortgage deed now in the British Museum, was executed on the following day. This, too, is signed by Shakespeare, Johnson, and Jackson. Heminges was again a participant. The mortgage was to ensure that Walker would receive a balance due of £60. Without possibility of question, the actor at the Globe and the gentleman from Stratford were the same man.

Shakespeare's will provides still more links with London. Each page is signed by him, and in it he makes bequests to three of his long-time friends of the London stage: "to my fellows John Heminge, Richard Burbage and Henry Condell twenty-six shillings, eight pence apiece to buy them rings." To Thomas Russell, Esq., he bequeathed £5 and entreated and appointed him to be one of the "overseers" of the will. Russell was a gentleman of good estate, who had inherited manors at Alderminster and Broad Campden, both within a few miles of Stratford-upon-Avon. He married, as his second wife, the widow of the great and wealthy scientist Thomas Digges, whose fine house was in the parish of St. Mary Aldermanbury in London. John Heminges was a fellow parishioner and later a churchwarden of St. Mary's. Russell came of an ancient family and had important relatives and friends. The younger of his stepsons, Leonard Digges, an Oxford graduate and a poet, was often at Stratford. His two poems in praise of Shakespeare take on greater importance from having been written by a man with every opportunity to know the dramatist personally. The shorter one, printed in the First Folio, gives the earliest reference to the memorial bust of Shakespeare in Holy Trinity Church.

To the Memory of the Deceased Author,
Master William Shakespeare.

Shakespeare, at length thy pious fellows give
The world thy works: thy works, by which outlive
Thy tomb thy name must; when that stone is rent,
And time dissolves thy Stratford monument,
Here we alive shall view thee still. This book,
When brass and marble fade, shall make thee look
Fresh to all ages.
    .   .   .   .   .
Be sure, our Shakespeare, thou canst never die,
But, crown'd with laurel, live eternally.
L. Digges

The longer poem, which was first printed with Shakespeare's *Poems* (1640), gives additional proof of personal knowledge of "never-dying Shakespeare":

First, that he was a poet none would doubt
That heard the applause of what he sees set out
Imprinted; . . .
Next Nature only helped him; for look thorough
This whole book, thou shalt find he doth not borrow
One phrase from Greeks, nor Latins imitate,
Nor once from vulgar languages translate,
Nor plagiary-like from others glean,
Nor begs he from each witty friend a scene
To piece his acts with; all that he doth write
Is pure his own. . . .

At Shakespeare's death it was thought that he should be buried in the Poets' Corner in Westminster Abbey alongside Chaucer, Spenser, and Francis Beaumont. One of the widely circulated poems of the time begins thus:

On Mr. Wm. Shakespeare he died in April 1616

Renowned Spenser, lie a thought more nigh
To learned Chaucer, and rare Beaumont lie
A little nearer Spenser, to make room
For Shakespeare. . . .

William Basse

John Milton realized that burying Shakespeare in Westminster Abbey would not have increased his fame. His poem "W. Shakespeare" in the Second Folio (1632) opens with these lines:

What needs my Shakespeare for his honor'd bones,
The labor of an age, in piled stones

.   .   .   .

Thou in our wonder and astonishment
Hast built thy self a lasting monument.

Milton is echoing Jonson's poem in the First Folio:

I will not lodge thee by
Chaucer or Spenser, or bid Beaumont lie
A little farther, to make thee a room:
Thou art a monument, without a tomb,
And art alive still, while thy book doth live.

But the actual "monument," the portrait bust in the chancel of Holy Trinity, has great importance. Erected before 1623, it was executed by the younger Gerard Johnson, son of the Dutch immigrant Gheerart Janssen, who carried on his business in London. Below the bust an inscription names Shakespeare and praises his writings. Above the cornice is a square block bearing the arms of Shakespeare. The inscription on the monument, in Latin and English, is itself a positive identification of Shakespeare as a poet.

27

Illus. 7. Shakespeare's memorial bust, Holy Trinity Church, Stratford-upon-Avon. Carved possibly from a life mask or a death mask, its acceptance and erection are fair assurances that the family considered it a reasonable likeness. Reproduced courtesy of the Trustees of the Shakespeare Birthplace Trust.

Iudicio Pylium, genio Socratem, arte Maronem:
Terra tegit, populus maeret, Olympus habet.

Stay, Passenger, why goest thou so fast?
Read, if thou canst, whom envious Death hath plast [placed]
Within this monument; Shakespeare, with whom
Quick nature died, whose name doth deck this tomb
Far more than cost. Sith all that he hath writ
Leaves living art but page to serve his wit
    Obiit Anno Domini 1616
    Ætatis 53, Die 23 April

The Latin verses may be rendered thus: "Him who was a
Nestor in wisdom, in intellect a Socrates, in art a Virgil, the
earth encloses, the people mourn, and Olympus holds."

The arms on the monument are depicted according to the
grant of arms issued on October 20, 1596, by the College of
Heralds. William Dethick, Garter Principal King of Arms,
drew up the document, of which two copies are in the official
files of the College of Heralds. In the upper lefthand corner,
opposite his first words, Dethick wrote Shakespeare's motto:
Non sanz droit, and made a drawing of his arms:

Gold, on a bend sables, a spear of the first steeled argent. And
for his crest or cognizance a falcon, his wings displayed argent,
standing on a wreath of his colors, supporting a spear gold, steeled
as aforesaid, set upon a helmet with mantles and tassels as hath
been accustomed and doth more plainly appear depicted on this
margin.

The arms on the Stratford monument agree in every detail
with Dethick's grant. They appear again on the seal of Susanna
Hall. There is no possibility that the family of the actor-poet
was not the recipient of the grant, because in the course of a
quarrel in 1602 among the heralds a paper was written which
names Shakespeare and gives a sketch of his arms; in the margin, apparently in the hand of Ralph Brooke, York Herald,
are the words: "Shakespeare the player." Another officer of

Illus. 8. A sketch of the coat of arms of "Shakespeare the player" as granted by William Dethick, Garter King of Arms, in 1596. Probably in the hand of Ralph Brooke, York Herald, about 1602. Folger MS V.a. 350.

30

the College of Heralds, the learned William Camden, author of the *Britannia* (1586) and of the *Annals* (1615) of Queen Elizabeth, and Clarenceux King of Arms, wrote as follows:

These may suffice for some poetical descriptions of our ancient poets; if I would come to our time, what a world could I present to you out of Sir Philip Sidney, Ed. Spenser, Samuel Daniel, Hugh Holland, Ben Jonson, Th. Campion, Mich. Drayton, George Chapman, John Marston, William Shakespeare, & other most pregnant wits of these our times. . . . [*Remains*, "Poets," 1605].

Within a few years of his death Shakespeare was bringing fame to Stratford. The unknown author of *A Banquet of Jests or Change of Cheer* (1630) begins a mildly amusing joke with words that illustrate the growth of Shakespeare's reputation: "One traveling through Stratford-upon-Avon, a town most remarkable for the birth of famous William Shakespeare . . ." A more detailed statement was written by a Lieutenant Hammond in 1634:

In that day's travel we came by Stratford-upon-Avon, where, in the Church in that town, there are some monuments; which Church was built by Archbishop Stratford; those worth observing and of which we took notice were these . . . a neat monument of that famous English poet, Mr. William Shakespeare, who was born here [*A Relation of a Short Survey of 26 Counties . . . By a Captain, a Lieutenant and an Ancient, All three of the Military Company of Norwich*].

In the year 1662 the Reverend Mr. John Ward, M.A. of Oxford in 1652, became rector of Holy Trinity Church. Upon leaving the university, Ward had taken lodgings in London near Barber Surgeon's Hall so that he might attend lectures on anatomy, for he was almost equally interested in the cure of the body and the cure of souls. His notebooks, now in the Folger Shakespeare Library, are filled with memoranda about medicine and theology and contain many references to events in his life and to people he met or heard about. They show that upon his arrival in Stratford he did what every prudent, conscientious clergyman does: he inquired about the important parishioners. One family name would interest him, for whenever he went into the chancel of Holy Trinity Church there was the monument to William Shakespeare, and there were the burial places of Anne his wife, Susanna his elder daughter, and her husband, the prominent physician Dr. John Hall.

Hall, the physician, a selection from whose casebooks had been translated into English and published in 1657, Ward would know about. Hall's daughter Elizabeth's first husband, Thomas Nash, was also buried in the chancel; she was in 1662 the wife of Sir John Bernard of Abingdon. Elizabeth had inherited New Place, one of the finest houses in Stratford, and, as all Stratford remembered, she and her mother had been hostesses in 1643 to Queen Henrietta Maria and her attendants when they occupied New Place en route from London to join King Charles in the North. Ward's notebooks contain six entries about Shakepeare and his family:

Shakespeare had but two daughters, one whereof Mr. Hall the physician married and by her had one daughter, to-wit the Lady Bernard of Abingdon:

I have heard that Mr. Shakespeare was a natural wit, without any art at all. He frequented the plays all his younger time, but in his elder days lived at Stratford; and supplied the stage with two plays every year, and for that had an allowance so large that he spent at the rate of a £1000 a year, as I have heard:

Remember to peruse Shakespeare's plays and be versed in them that I may not be ignorant in that matter:

Shakespeare, Drayton, and Ben Jonson had a merry meeting and it seems drank too hard, for Shakespeare died of a fever there contracted. [It has been conjectured that he caught pneumonia, for drinking does not cause a fever.]

The testimony of the Reverend Mr. John Ward is unimpeachable. The most famous names in recent Stratford history

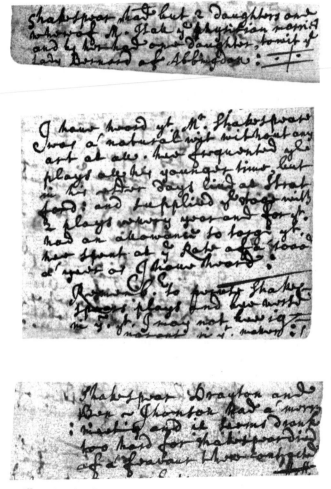

Illus. 9. The four references to Shakespeare in the John Ward Notebooks (*ca.* 1647–*ca.* 1680) quoted on page 32. These references quoted appear in Folger MS V.a. 292, ff. 138v, 140r, and 150r. The two references not quoted are in V.a. 294, f. 21r and V.a. 295, f. 120r.

were Shakespeare and Hall. The most exciting event in recent memory was the visit of Queen Henrietta Maria. Shakespeare's granddaughter was now Lady Bernard, and the family home was one of the show places of the town. Of course the new rector must read Shakespeare's plays, so as not to show ignorance of them, for apparently they were part of the subject of conversation among the best people.

There are two authentic likenesses of Shakespeare. One of these is the engraving by Martin Droeshout, printed on the title page of the First Folio (1623). Since the artist was only about twenty-two when the book came from the press, he must have worked from a portrait; at the age of fifteen, as he was when the poet died, he was too young to have formed a trustworthy impression. The identity of the portrait he copied is unknown. Possibly it was that now in the National Portrait Gallery in London. This has been attributed to Richard Burbage, who is known to have painted portraits; it has also been attributed to Joseph Taylor, an actor with the King's Men (or to John Taylor, a contemporary artist). According to early tradition, Taylor bequeathed it to Shakespeare's godson, Sir William Davenant. From him it passed to Thomas Betterton. From Betterton it went to his long-time associate on the stage, Mrs. Barry. The record of its ownership continues unbroken until it became the property of the Duke of Chandos, from whom it passed to the National Portrait Gallery. Whatever faults of execution Droeshout may have committed in his engraving, it is certain that Shakespeare's friends provided him with an authentic portrait to copy.

The portrait bust in Stratford was erected in 1622. Gerard Johnson the Younger carved it, possibly from a life mask or a death mask. Its acceptance and erection in Holy Trinity Church are reasonable assurances that the family considered it a reasonable likeness. About 1748 it required minor repairs and repainting. Later, in 1793, it was painted stone color to give it a classical appearance. And still later, in 1861, the original colors were restored as faithfully as might be. Because of differences in detail in the engraving printed in William Dugdale's *Warwickshire* (1656), there has been controversy about the reliability of the bust as it is now seen. This need not be taken seriously, for many of the monuments depicted by Dugdale, unchanged from his day to this, differ markedly from the engravings in *Warwickshire*. It may be remarked that Dugdale shows the arms of Shakespeare, as granted by Dethick in 1596, and the inscription below the bust which names the poet.

When interest in Shakespeare caused collectors to buy early quartos and folios at ever higher prices, it was natural that a search should be made for early portraits. Some of those brought to light may be genuine likenesses, painted in his lifetime, but not one has an unbroken pedigree, and so all are suspect. Others, when subjected to close study, have proved to be clumsy or skillful alterations of early portraits of subjects unknown. The market for Shakespeare portraits was brisk, buyers were not always critical, and false claims were made. This kind of shady business has nothing to do with the authorship of Shakespeare; it is simply proof that a painting called "Shakespeare" would fetch a higher price than a "portrait of a gentleman unknown."

The Elizabethan indifference to playwrights extended to their manuscripts. Manuscript plays had value only for actors, who might want to perform them, or publishers, who might want to have them printed. There were no Elizabethan collectors of literary autographs. When Francis Bacon arranged with Humfrey Hooper to publish his *Essays* in 1597, Hooper delivered the manuscript to John Windet the printer, and when the job was finished, this manuscript was discarded. No one treasured it, not even the author. By 1625 the number of Bacon's essays had increased in successive editions from ten to fifty-eight. If Bacon had been a man of relatively small importance in 1597, he had risen meteorically under King James until he became Baron Verulam, Viscount St. Alban, and Lord Chancellor; then meteorlike he had fallen. Had Elizabethans been collectors of literary autographs, surely the manuscripts of the successive revisions of and additions to the *Essays* should have been a prize worth striving for. But no one was interested, and in consequence Bacon's manuscripts of the *Essays* perished. In just the same way Shakespeare's holograph copies of *Venus and Adonis* and *The Rape of Lucrece* were discarded as waste paper as soon as Richard Field had set them in type.

As a matter of fact, paper was an expensive commodity and was seldom wasted. Almost all the paper was imported, and people used it until it went to pieces. The bindings of Elizabethan books are filled with scraps of manuscript and pieces of printed matter that accumulated in the shops of printers and bookbinders. All that is left of the first edition of Shakespeare's *King Henry IV, Part I,* is a single sheet, now in the Folger Shakespeare Library, that someone used in making a binding for a copy of Thomas' *Rules of the Italian Grammar* (1567). As late as 1700 a favorite way to insult a poet was to suggest that his verses would be good for lighting a fire or wrapping a fish, or for some humbler use.

Very few of the plays written in Tudor and early Stuart times were printed. The actors believed that popular plays should be kept out of print, for if people could buy and read them they might be less eager to pay to see performances in the theatre. Another danger was that rival companies of actors might use them for giving performances, for there was no law to prevent such competition.

Then, as now, a playwright sold his new play to a producer, who was in Shakespeare's age a company of actors. The modern playwright may, if he wishes, retain publishing, radio, television, and moving picture rights. Not so in Elizabethan times. When a company of actors bought a play, it acquired all rights. The company could perform the play as written or employ someone to revise it; it could even lock up the play without performance; it could, at its discretion, sell the play to a publisher. The publisher, in turn, acquired absolute copyright to himself and his heirs forever. When he had the play printed, it did not occur to him to ask or permit the author to read proofs, for in selling his play to the actors the author had disposed of all his rights in it. In Shakespeare's case he sold his plays, after 1594, to the company of which he was a sharer. The manuscripts went into what may be called the company library, and there the licensed promptbooks presumably remained until Parliament closed all playhouses in 1642 and the King's Men distributed their assets among the then sharers.

The other companies of actors may be presumed to have parceled out their play manuscripts in the same way in 1642. Several promptbooks, such as Philip Massinger's *The City Madam*, were sold to publishers or published by their unemployed actor-owners. By 1653 Humphrey Moseley, the publisher, had bought up from the actors a quantity of manuscript plays that had never been printed and entered them in the Stationers' Register. Only a few of these were printed, because the London of the Commonwealth period had little love for the stage; many of the manuscripts have disappeared. Probably the Great Fire of 1666 took a heavy toll of unprinted plays as it swept through London and destroyed untold quantities of bookshops and their contents. (Copies of the Third Folio of Shakespeare of 1663/1664 are scarce for the probable reason that many of the unsold copies were burned.)

It was not until about 1660 that private collectors appear to have developed an interest in unprinted plays. A letter from the Lords Somerset, Cavendish (later the Duke of Devonshire, builder of Chatsworth), Gerard, and Roscommon contains greetings to a wealthy fellow collector, Abraham Hill. Cavendish, along with the Earls of Oxford, Pembroke, Winchilsea, and Sunderland and others of lower station, made regular Saturday excursions to the shops in quest of rare books and manuscripts. And about 1678 Hill copied down the titles of more than fifty manuscript plays he had come upon. Only three plays are now extant in manuscript with titles corresponding to those in Hill's list; no manuscripts of the other plays are traceable.

There is no reference to Shakespeare's play manuscripts in his will for the obvious reason that he no longer possessed them. As written, each had been sold to the actors.

During Shakespeare's life approximately half of his plays were put into print in one way or another; sometimes from unauthorized manuscripts, as in the case of the first quartos of *Romeo and Juliet, Hamlet, Henry V,* and others; sometimes from copies that seem to have been in Shakespeare's own handwriting, as *The Merchant of Venice* or the second quarto of *Romeo and Juliet.* When the printer finished his job, the manuscripts were regarded as worthless. The same thing happened after Jaggard had finished printing the Folio of 1623; the printer's copy was thrown away. This tossing out of printer's copy was not peculiar to Shakespeare. Of all the hundreds of plays put in print up to 1700, there is not one surviving example of a manuscript that went through a print shop. Obviously the nonsurvival of Shakespearean literary manuscripts has no bearing on the subject of authorship.

Letters and private papers, except the real estate documents referred to above, have all disappeared. At Shakespeare's death they would have remained in New Place in the care of his widow Anne and his elder daughter Susanna Hall. After the death of the widow in 1623 Dr. John Hall and his wife remained at New Place. Hall's will, probated in 1636, provided that his "Study of Books" (these may or may not have included volumes belonging to Shakespeare) should be disposed of as his son-in-law Thomas Nash might wish: "As for my manuscripts . . . you may, son Nash, burn them or do with them what you please." In consequence of a lawsuit against Dr. Hall and his heirs, a charge was filed in 1637 by Susanna Hall, her daughter Elizabeth, and the latter's husband, Thomas Nash, that in August, 1636, Baldwyn Brookes, mercer of Stratford, with the assistance of the undersheriff and some of the Stratford officers, broke into New Place and "there did take and seize upon the ready money, books, goods, and chattels of the said John Hall deceased . . . to the value of one thousand pounds at the least and have converted the same to their or some of their own uses without inventorying or appraising the same." No further documents in the suit have been discovered, and so it is not known whether Mistress Hall recovered anything.

At the death, in 1670, of Shakespeare's last lineal descendant, his granddaughter Elizabeth, it may be supposed that any surviving books and papers remained at Abingdon, the residence of her second husband, Sir John Bernard.

There are several books in which Shakespeare's name is written. Some of the signatures may be genuine, but others are obvious forgeries.

As Shakespeare's plays gained ever wider popularity, some of their admirers expressed their admiration in extravagant terms. Idolaters professed to find technical knowledge about law, medicine, military science, and the like that is ordinarily possessed only by professionals, together with familiarity with foreign lands betokening wide travel, and erudition and elegance suitable to university-educated members of the nobility. No human ever possessed all the qualities that were in sum attributed to Shakespeare. In reaction against these absurdities, first one and then another writer began to point out the discrepancies between the biographical facts then known and the supposed accomplishments. The next stage was to propose that someone else wrote the plays.

Reduced to simplest terms, the process was as follows: The plays must have been written by a learned man, an intimate of the court, who had traveled extensively. Who had these qualifications? The first name to be proposed was that of Francis Bacon, who in youth had "taken all knowledge to be [his] province." Other people, dissatisfied with this candidate, suggested Edward de Vere, seventeenth Earl of Oxford, or Henry Wriothesley, third Earl of Southampton, or William Stanley, sixth Earl of Derby, until twenty or more rivals were in the field, including Queen Elizabeth I and Anne Hathaway. When each of these, in turn, was proved by opposed partisans to be ineligible, it was argued that a coterie wrote the plays and poems, or that the works had been parceled out to a number of people. In no case has it been possible to produce a shred of evidence that anyone in Shakespeare's day questioned his authorship. And not one fact has been discovered to prove that anyone but Shakespeare was the author.

It may be well to classify the objections to William Shakespeare and consider them apart from the claims advanced for any of the proposed authors.

The bitter attacks on Shakespeare often begin by calling Stratford-upon-Avon a mean, dirty, bookless town, incapable of producing a great man. The facts are that Stratford was a prosperous borough town with an ancient charter, where citizens were not merely renters but were the owners of their homes. The charge that Stratford was dirty proceeds out of a single item in the borough accounts: the record of a fine levied upon John Shakespeare for permitting a heap of refuse to collect before his house in 1552. The commendable zeal of the authorities in enforcing their regulations is the best evidence that Stratford had standards of sanitation and took vigorous measures to uphold them. The grammar school had been conducted for two hundred years before the Reformation and customarily employed Oxford and Cambridge graduates at high salaries. This "proper little market town," as William Camden the historian described it, was capable of producing important men. John de Stratford, who enlarged the parish church and founded a college of priests nearby, rose to the Archbishopric of Canterbury in the reign of Edward III, and his brother Robert became Bishop of Chichester and Chancellor of England. Another son of Stratford, Sir Hugh Clopton, was Lord Mayor of London in the year Columbus discovered America. Sir Hugh built the stone bridge that is still used by traffic crossing the Avon; he also built the nave of the Guild Chapel, still a landmark in Stratford; and the house he erected in 1483, New Place, became in due time the residence of William Shakespeare. Clopton's will provided funds for what would now be called five-year scholarships to six poor boys, three at Oxford and three at Cambridge.

The second charge brought against Shakespeare is ignorance. He has been called, among other things, "the mean, drunken, ignorant and absolutely unlettered rustic of Stratford," who could neither read nor write a line. Some people, after trying to decipher the signatures to Shakespeare's will and other legal documents have, in their own ignorance, called him illiterate. The usual hand written in England from about 1500 until long after Shakespeare's death bears the name of English or secretary. The "fine Italian hand" that Shakespeare mentions was introduced in the sixteenth century and by 1700 it had almost completely displaced the secretary hand. English or secretary letters resemble those used in German script, and most of them are totally different from the familiar italic letters of the modern cursive hand. Once the secretary forms are learned, Elizabethan manuscripts are no more or less difficult to read than modern hands. It is just as proper to call Goethe illiterate for writing German script as to say that Shakespeare was illiterate because he wrote English or secretary script.

The nature and extent of Shakespeare's schooling has already been described, as has the extent of formal education exhibited in the plays. The poet laureate John Dryden, a "learned" poet of the reign of Charles II, sums up the situation neatly in his *Of Dramatic Poesy, An Essay:*

To begin, then, with Shakespeare: he was the man who of all modern, and perhaps ancient poets, had the largest and most comprehensive soul. All the images of nature were still present to him, and he drew them not laboriously, but luckily: when he describes anything, you more than see it, you feel it too. Those who accuse him to have wanted learning, give him the greater commendation: he was naturally learn'd; he needed not the spectacles of books to read nature, he look'd inwards, and found her there.

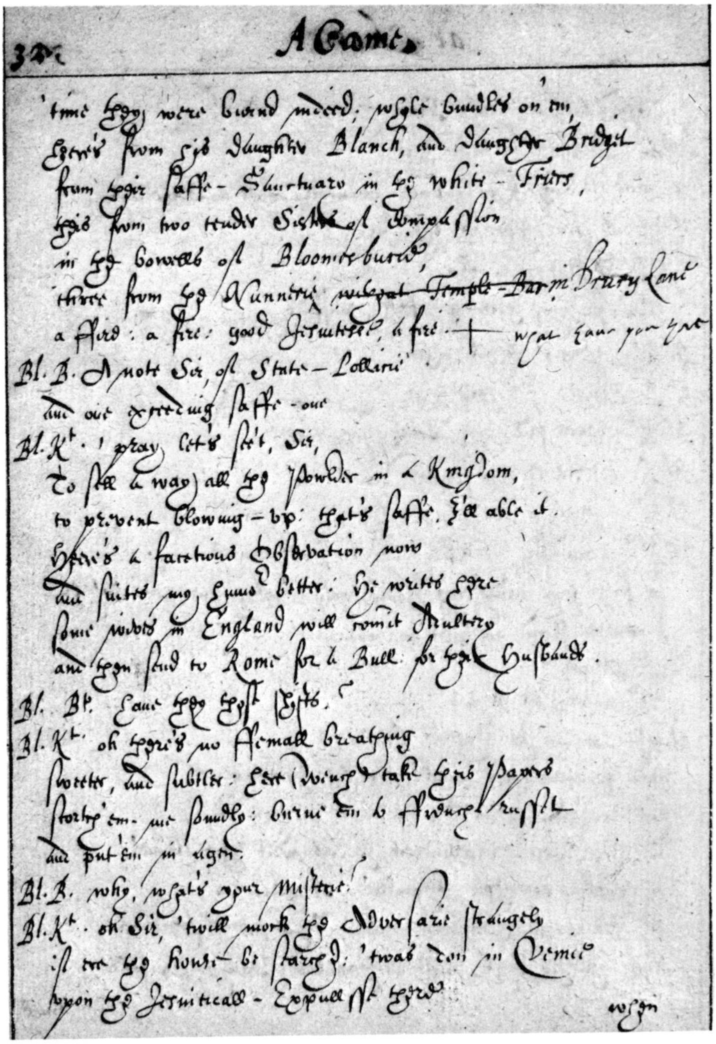
32 A Game.

'time they were burnd indeed; whole bundles on 'em,
theres from his daughter Blanch, and daughter Bridget
from their safe-Sanctuarie in the white-Friers,
this from two tender Sisters of Compassion
in the bowells of Bloomesburie,
three from the Nunnerie ~~in the Temple-Bar~~ in Drury Lane
a fire: a fire: good Jesuite, a fire. What haue you there?
Bl. B. A note Sir, of State-Policie
and our exceeding safe-one
Bl. Kt. I pray let's see't, Sir,
To sell away all the powder in a Kingdom,
to prevent blowing-vp: that's safe, Ile able it.
Here's a facetious Observation now
and suites my humor better: he writes here
some wives in England will commit Adulterie
and then send to Rome for a Bull for their Husbands.
Bl. B. haue they those shifts?
Bl. Kt. oh there's no smell breathing
sweeter, and subtler: Heere (Wench) take these Papers
scorch 'em and soundly: burne 'em to fine russet
and put 'em in again.
Bl. B. why, what's your Misterie?
Bl. Kt. oh Sir, 'twill work the Adversarie strangely
if we the house be searcht: 'twas don in Venice
vpon the Jesuiticall-Expulsion there
when

Illus. 10. A page of Thomas Middleton's *A Game at Chess* (1624), in the handwriting of Ralph Crane, who did professional copying for the King's Men. In lines 6 and 7 the author, a younger contemporary of Shakespeare, has made corrections in the text. Predominantly in secretary hand with some place names and individual letters in italic ("Italian hand"). Folger MS V.a. 231.

A third objection to Shakespeare is that he could have had no opportunity to hear the conversation of royalty and nobility and, consequently, could not have written the dialogue of the plays. But just how did royalty and the nobility talk? Where are the transcripts of councils, private conversations, and amorous courtship? A modern poet (Don Marquis in "Pete the Parrot and Shakespeare") has a manager hand Shakespeare a "mouldy old script" and demand that he prepare at once a manuscript filled with some of his usual hokum: fat men making love, "and kings talking like kings never had sense enough to talk." The fact is that Shakespeare's court scenes are psychologically convincing, and we assume that people in the Renaissance actually talked in this way. If it were true that only courtiers could write dialogue like that, John Webster, the son of a London merchant tailor, must have been an Italian courtier to write the effective dialogue of his plays *The White Devil* and *The Duchess of Malfi*.

Several of Shakespeare's plays include details that have not yet been traced in source books and appear to suggest firsthand observation of foreign places and customs. Thus *Love's Labor's Lost* shows more than casual familiarity with French names. *The Two Gentlemen of Verona* has unusual geographic details. Some knowledge of Elsinore is supposed to be revealed in *Hamlet* and possession of then unprinted historical details in *Macbeth*. Now Bacon or the Earl of Derby might be proposed as the authors of *Love's Labor's Lost* because of their travels in France. The Earl of Rutland had an embassage to Denmark, a fact not overlooked by those who would assign *Hamlet* to him. A reputed journey to Italy by the Earl of Southampton encourages some writers to think he wrote *The Two Gentlemen of Verona*. Plays have been attributed on similar grounds to the Earl of Essex, Sir Walter Raleigh, and others. Even if one single piece of evidence could be found to support any or all of these various ascriptions, the results would be chaotic, for it would be necessary to believe that a coterie composed of these, and perhaps other, people wrote the plays.

That is, of course, absurd. Some of these men were the bitterest rivals and at times deadly enemies. It is inconceivable that for a period of about twenty-five years (1588–1612) they could have collaborated to produce the plays at the dates they are known to have appeared on the stage. To hold such opinions is to shut one's eyes to the many sources of information open to a playwright. Even an island-bound poet could talk to travelers, who brought back stories from France and Italy and vivid accounts of their cities and customs. News pamphlets taught Londoners the names of the principal leaders in the French Wars, if only because English treasure was invested in the cause of Henry of Navarre and because the outcome of that religious struggle was of vital importance to every Englishman. English actors, reputed to be the best in Europe, performed frequently in Denmark, as well as in Germany and the Netherlands, and they reported their observations and experiences to all who would listen. Shakespeare's Romans are as truly Roman as his Renaissance Italians are Italian. No one, on this account, would suggest that the author of *Julius Caesar* must have lived in ancient Rome. The truth of the matter is that poetic genius overleaps both space and time.

The author of the plays was not a formally trained lawyer—or doctor, or soldier, or sailor—however vividly and appropriately technical terms are often used. Research has shown that Shakespeare uses legal terms and situations less frequently than some of the other playwrights, and often less accurately. It was a litigious age. People haled each other into court upon small provocation, and a certain number of legal terms made up a part of every man's vocabulary. So with war and navigation. A sword or dagger was never very far from an Elizabethan's hand. The citizenry were expected to know something of the use of weapons. And the average Londoner was much closer to the sea in those days of Drake and Hawkins and Frobisher than today. What a poet needed was a quick eye, a keen ear, a sensitive imagination, and a retentive memory—

and, in Dryden's words, "the largest and most comprehensive soul of all modern, and perhaps ancient poets."

Most of the objections to Shakespeare as the author of his plays have originated in ignorance of theatrical conditions and of the records that have survived. Frequently it is stated, for example, that Shakespeare could not have been a playwright because his name does not appear in the records of Philip Henslowe. Henslowe was a London businessman with a variety of interests. He engaged in pawnbroking, invested in real estate, was active in bearbaiting, and held minor court appointments; but his name lives because of the contents of his theatrical account books. Between 1592 and his death in 1616 he owned or financed several playhouses (the Rose, the theatre at Newington Butts, the Fortune, the Hope) and had financial dealings with, or was banker for, several companies of actors (chiefly the Admiral's Men, 1594–1604; then Worcester's, the Lady Elizabeth's, etc.) His *Diary* and *Papers,* as the account books are called, are among the most detailed and valuable records of the Elizabethan theatre. They contain, among other matters, many entries of payments to Jonson, Dekker, Hathaway, Drayton, and others for writing plays. Shakespeare's name is not mentioned. Why? The answer is easy. In the early 1590's theatrical people were in a turmoil. Acting companies formed, disintegrated, and reformed, with much shifting about of actors and sale and resale of promptbooks. The plague closed the playhouses for much of the time between 1592 and 1594, with occasional brief intervals of theatrical activity. Several titles of Shakespearean interest appear in Henslowe's business records for these years: *Henry VI, Titus Andronicus, Taming of the Shrew, Hamlet.* But at this time Henslowe did not name the authors of plays, and so it is not possible to match plays and poets.

In the autumn of 1594 relief from the plague permitted the resumption of theatrical activity in London. And just at this time the Lord Chamberlain took under his protection a newly

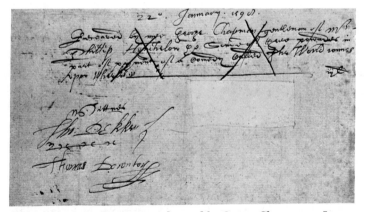

Illus. 11(a). A note, written and signed by Thomas Dekker, for £3 loaned to him by Philip Henslowe on January 18, 1598. Thomas Downton and Edward Juby, two actors, sign as witnesses. One side of Folger MS X.d. 319.

Illus. 11(b). A receipt written and signed by George Chapman on January 22, 1598, for £3 from Philip Henslowe, in part payment—in advance—for writing a play called *The World Runs upon Wheels.* Chapman's signature has been cut out by an autograph collector. Thomas Dekker and Thomas Downton sign as witnesses. The other side of Folger MS X.d. 319.

organized company of actors that included William Shakespeare. From 1594 until the playhouses were closed in 1642 this company had a continuous history, with a succession of noble patrons until 1603, when King James chose them to be the King's Men. During the long years from 1594 to 1642 this company was, almost without interruption, the strongest, best, and most successful in London, as the record of payments to them for performances at Court clearly demonstrates. Not once in these years did Shakespeare's company have any financial connections with Philip Henslowe or with any of the acting companies dependent upon him. Since after 1594 Shakespeare acted and wrote only for the company of which he had become a sharer, his name could not appear in Henslowe's records, any more than the president of General Motors could be named on the payrolls of Chrysler or Ford.

Much ingenuity has been expended in the attempt to find in Shakespeare's works hidden messages about their authorship, and there is a voluminous literature on the subject. This has all been subjected to impartial scrutiny by two eminent cryptanalysts, William F. and Elizebeth S. Friedman, who in *The Shakespearean Ciphers Examined* (1957) prove conclusively that no crypto-system hitherto used by anti-Shakespeareans meets the basic tests of cryptology. Determined to avoid partisanship, they refuse to make a search for codes or ciphers, but they give assurance that none of the supposed discoveries thus far reported has any validity.

Shakespeare's artistry, unique in its perfection, did not develop in a vacuum. The Shakespeare of the early plays sounds, for lines on end, like Marlowe or Greene or Kyd or Peele, because these men had slightly preceded him in the field and had something he could learn by imitation. Then Heywood and Middleton and a dozen others, slightly younger, began to learn from Shakespeare. Theatrical London of those years was an exciting, intoxicating little world, somewhat like New York and Hollywood in the early days of radio and television. Everyone tried to improve on everything that had succeeded for anyone else, and then to invent something new. Writers imitated, they borrowed, each man learning from the others and, with luck, doing something original that the rest would try to copy. At the same time they ridiculed and criticized each other, so that the exact date of a play can sometimes be arrived at by a study of the plays it imitates or borrows from and those that, in turn, imitate or satirize it. These things were true of diction and metrics, as well as of incident, character, and plot. So it is relatively easy to write the history of English drama from, say, 1585 to 1642. The events hang together, with a place for everyone and everyone in his place. In such a scheme the observed development of Shakespeare as theatrical writer and poet is credible and logical. The chronology of his works meshes perfectly with the chronology of the whole literature of the age.

There is no problem of authorship for those who have read Elizabethan drama in a setting of Elizabethan literature and history. Those who find difficulty do so because they attempt to treat Shakespeare as a special case, without proper reference to contemporary writers and the customs and attitudes of his age. Read Shakespeare's works in chronological order of composition, and it will be obvious that they are the product of a single intellect. Metrical devices, characteristics of expression, qualities of mind that are present in the earliest writings, are traceable throughout. But as the poet develops, his early exuberance changes to skillful mastery and ripens into mature profundity. The early comedies tinkle with rhyme and sparkle with wordplay as the poet revels in the discovery of his talent. The golden comedies and the late histories reveal a writer who has mastered his craft and is free to contemplate the vanities of "Man, proud Man." The next stage of development is to investigate some of the complexities of the human spirit and to grapple with the timeless problems of evil and death. At length come the romances, in which the poet is concerned with forgiveness and reconciliation and the renewal of life. Throughout, there is the same mind at work, revealing itself in the careful architecture of the plays. Throughout, there is the same sensitive spirit, able to enter perfectly into the mind and heart of every character in every situation. And throughout, there is the same incredible mastery of language, so that each character always has the right words to express his particular thought or emotion.

> Nature herself was proud of his designs,
>   And joy'd to wear the dressing of his lines! . . .
> Yet must I not give Nature all, Thy art,
>   My gentle Shakespeare, must enjoy a part.
> For though the poet's matter, Nature be,
>   His art doth give the fashion. . . .
> For a good poet's made, as well as born.
>   And such wert thou.

> [Ben Jonson, "To the Memory of My Beloved, the Author Mr. William Shakespeare: and What He Hath Left Us," prefixed to the First Folio, 1623].

SUGGESTED READING

The life of Shakespeare may be studied in great detail in Sir Edmund Chambers' *William Shakespeare: A Study of Facts and Problems* (2 vols., Oxford, 1930), an encyclopedic presentation of biographical and literary documents and criticism, with a good bibliography of each topic. A much more readable account will be found in *A Life of William Shakespeare* (Boston, 1923) by Joseph Quincy Adams. Marchette Chute's *Shakespeare of London* (New York, 1949; reissued as a paperback in 1957) is a lively story of Shakespeare as a human being, particularly valuable for its account of other members of Shakespeare's company, such as Heminges and Condell. Excellent short biographies will be found in Giles E. Dawson's *The Life of William Shakespeare* (Folger Booklets on Tudor and Stuart Civilization, Washington, 1958) and the sections entitled "The Author," "The Publication of His Plays," and "The Shakespearean Theatre" by Louis B. Wright in the Introductions to the several volumes of The Folger Library General Reader's Shakespeare (New York, in progress).

The borough accounts of Stratford-upon-Avon contain the records of John Shakespeare and give a fair picture of the status of that busy market town (Edgar I. Fripp, editor, *Minutes and Accounts of the Corporation of Stratford-upon-Avon and Other Records, 1553–1620,* transcribed by Richard Savage (4 vols., Oxford, 1921–). Levi Fox has written a readable, well-illustrated history of Stratford, *The Borough Town of Stratford-upon-Avon* (Stratford-upon-Avon, 1953).

A brief account of education in Shakespeare's time will be found in Craig R. Thompson's *Schools in Tudor England* (Folger Booklets on Tudor and Stuart Civilization, Washington, 1958). *The Education of Shakespeare* (London and New York, 1933) by George R. Plimpton gives an account of some of the important schoolbooks of that period. Detailed discussions of the school curriculums and the influence of schoolbooks on Shakespeare will be found in T. W. Baldwin's *William Shakspere's Petty School* (Urbana, Ill., 1943) and his *William Shakspere's Small Latine and Lesse Greeke* (Urbana, Ill., 1944). Virgil K. Whitaker's *Shakespeare's Use of Learning* (San Marino, Calif., 1953) deals with the reflections of Shakespeare's reading in some of his works. And Sister Miriam Joseph's *Shakespeare's Use of the Arts of Language* is a technical treatise on the rhetorical devices Shakespeare learned in school.

The best source of information about play manuscripts and theatrical documents is the generously illustrated *Dramatic Documents from the Elizabethan Playhouses; Stage Plots; Actors' Parts; Prompt Books* (2 vols., Oxford, 1931) by Sir Walter Greg. "Where Are Shakespeare's Manuscripts?" (*New Colophon,* no. 8 [1950], pp. 357–369) by James G. McManaway, is a popular description of some of the conditions in which an Elizabethan playwright worked. There is a mine of information about Elizabethan theatrical conditions in *Henslowe's Diary* (2 vols., London, 1904–1908) and *Henslowe Papers* (London, 1907), both edited by Sir Walter Greg. R. A. Foakes and R. T. Rickert have just published a new edition, *Henslowe's Diary . . . with Supplementary Material* (Cambridge, Eng., 1961), from a fresh transcription of Henslowe's manuscripts. An excellent idea about how plays were licensed before performance is given in Joseph Q. Adams' *The Dramatic Records of Sir Henry Herbert, Master of the Revels, 1623–1673* (New Haven, 1917). This is brought up to date in Adams' essay, "The Office-Book of Sir Henry Herbert, Master of the Revels" (in *To Doctor R.* [Philadelphia, 1953], pp. 1–9). The most extensive collection of literary autograph material is Sir Walter Greg's *English Literary Autographs, 1550–1650* (Oxford, 1932, issued in three parts), which reproduces specimens of the handwriting of poets and playwrights, with transcripts, and lists all the examples known to him in 1932 to have survived. This is invaluable for learning what manuscripts written in English secretary look like. A slightly earlier study, without facsimiles, describes the scarcity of writing in the hands of Elizabethan playwrights, "Extant Autograph Material by Shakespeare's Fellow Dramatists" (*The Library*, ser. 4, X [1930], 308–312) by Henrietta C. Bartlett. The most detailed study of Shakespeare's handwriting and of his probable part in *Sir Thomas More* is *Shakespeare's Hand in "Sir Thomas More"* (Cambridge, Eng., 1923) by Alfred W. Pollard, Sir Walter Greg, E. Maunde Thompson, J. Dover Wilson, and R. W. Chambers. This reproduces portions of the manuscript play supposed to be in Shakespeare's handwriting and each of the six signatures of Shakespeare preserved on legal documents.

The early allusions to Shakespeare as an actor, poet, and playwright and the hundreds of imitations or echoes of his lines and references to his dramatis personae are collected in *The Shakspere Allusion Book: A Collection of Allusions to Shakspere from 1591 to 1700* (reissued, 2 vols., Oxford, 1932). In a preface to the reprint Sir Edmund Chambers adds a few important allusions discovered in recent years. He gives a judicious selection of the allusions in appendixes to his *William Shakespeare*. Gerald E. Bentley adds a number of allusions in *Shakespeare and Jonson: Their Reputations in the Seventeenth Century Compared* (2 vols., Chicago, 1945) and points out that references tend to praise the learning and art of Jonson at the expense of Shakespeare, the natural genius.

The most careful study of Shakespeare portraits is that of M. H. Spielmann, *The Title-Page of the First Folio of Shakespeare's Plays: A Comparative Study of the Droeshout Portrait and the Stratford Monument* (London, 1924).

R. C. Churchill, *Shakespeare and His Betters* (Bloomington, Ind., 1958), Frank W. Wadsworth, *The Poacher from Stratford* (Berkeley, Calif., 1958), and H. N. Gibson, *The Shakespeare Claimants: A Critical Survey of the Four Principal Theories concerning the Authorship of the Shakespearean Plays* (London, New York, 1962), have collected information about the history of anti-Shakespeareanism and the chief anti-Stratfordians. "The Anti-Shakespeare Industry and the Growth of Cults" by Louis B. Wright (*Virginia Quarterly Review*, XXV [1959], 289–303) is a spirited attack upon faddist speculation. James G. McManaway discusses the matter from a different point of view in "Shakespeare and the Heretics" (*To Doctor R.* [Philadelphia, 1953], pp. 136–153). And there is a considered account by Giles E. Dawson in "The Anti-Shakespearean Theories" (*Encyclopaedia Britannica*, XX [1960–], 457–458).

The claims of those who have sought acrostic or code and cipher messages in Shakespeare's works are considered and rejected as illusory by Colonel William F. Friedman and Mrs. Friedman in *The Shakespearean Ciphers Examined* (Cambridge, Eng., 1957).

PR 2937 .M3 1979
McManaway, James C.
The authorship of
 Shakespeare